AF413244

Alex ran into the kitchen. "What's for dinner Mom?"

"Chicken" said Mom

"And what else?" said Alex

"Rice" said Mom

"And what else?" said Alex

"String Beans" said Mom

"String Beans make me strong!" said Alex

"What else is for dinner Mom?"

"Rolls with butter" said Mom

"And what else" said Alex

"That's all" said Mom

"I don't like it!" said Alex

"Well then, I guess you won't like this cake that I baked" said Mom

"OK, I will eat it! But..."

"Tomorrow, can we have hotdogs for dinner?" said Alex

"And what else?" said Mom

The End